Capture the Flag

William D. Van Atta Jr.

Dedication

To my mom, dad, three brothers and three sisters for all their loving support over the years. To the many precious furry and winged companions, I have had the honor of experiencing life with.

Acknowledgment

I would like to give special thanks to my mom who introduced me to the poems of her grandfather, Joseph Russell Taylor and his acquaintance, Robert W. Service. Thank you to the many teachers who patiently helped me with my deficient reading and writing skills.

For introducing me to north woods I would like to thank the Whiteway's, Dr. Robert (Red) and wife Marion. I worked my way through college as the Whiteway's handy man.

About the Author

William (Bill) D. Van Atta Jr. is a veteran Army aviator and retired registered nurse. A native of the Midwest, he now resides in La Crescent, Minnesota. Bill holds a Bachelor of Science degree in Geography from the University of Wisconsin–La Crosse.

After serving 12 years in the U.S. Army as both a rotary-wing and fixed-wing aviator, Bill returned to school and graduated from The Norfolk General Hospital School of Nursing. He went on to complete his Bachelor of Science in Nursing at Excelsior University and became a licensed RN.

Bill practiced in several hospitals, including Level 1 and Level 2 trauma centers, where he specialized in the care of surgical, trauma, and burn patients.

When he's not writing, Bill enjoys spending time with his dogs. He especially likes being outdoors—camping, hiking, and photographing nature. In recent years, he has also been putting his woodworking skills to the test by building a small sailboat. An avid swimmer, Bill has competed in several open-water swimming competitions.

You can connect with Bill at: running_wolf57@yahoo.com

Just another day in God's country for a 12-year-old boy or so it seemed. It was a brisk spring day in late May 1970, still half asleep, 1 was up getting ready for school. For breakfast, a piece of peanut butter, and jelly toast and a glass of orange juice. Then off to school on my one speed Schwinn bicycle.

I was a student at the Campus School on the grounds of the University of Wisconsin -La Crosse. The school, grades K through 9, occupied what is now Morris Hall on the southwest side of the campus.

I lived about 3 blocks from the school, so the bike ride was a short one. North on 17th Place to Main, then a left turn, right turn, another left on State Street and there I was. I secured my bike in the bike rack among the assortment of bicycles one of them a beautiful new five speed stingray with a banana seat and high-rise handlebars. I eyed the bike then scurried into the school.

I don't remember what grade I was in, but I guess I could figure it out if I strained my brain enough. I do however remember the day very well, sometimes with mixed feelings especially knowing more about what led to the events influencing the day.

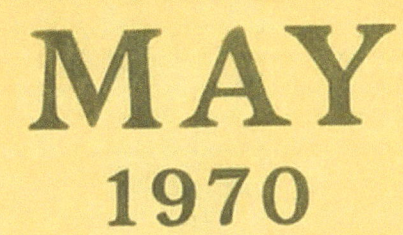

MAY
1970

S	M	T	W	T	F	S
				1	2	3	4
5	6	7	8	9	10	11
12	13	14	15	16	17	18
19	20	21	22	23	24	25
26	27	28	29	30	31	

Sitting at my desk daydreaming I was awakened by the bell. The school day began, as always, standing, hand on heart facing the flag and reciting the pledge of allegiance.

I never really liked school I just figured it was another part of life that one had to endure. The day was progressing slowly. We trudged through one subject after another until it was time for a few minutes on the playground.

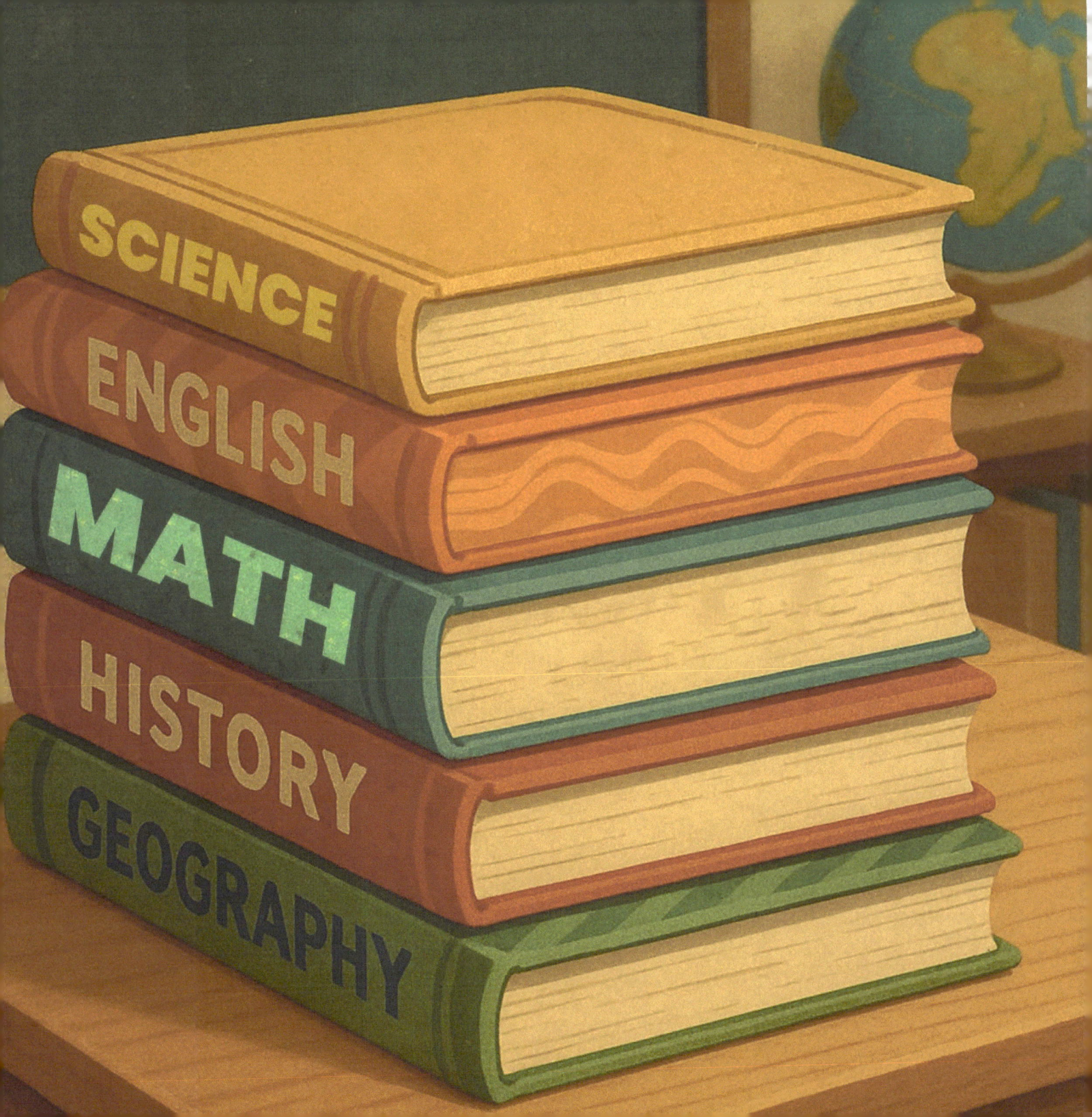

We paraded down the stairs in orderly fashion and out the doors, then we ran like crazy to the playground for a game of kickball. It was then that we noticed something was different. Several college students had left class and were protesting the war. I still have the image in my head of one protester whose dog had a peace sign shaved into its fur and highlighted with florescent pink paint. The protesters were noisy but peaceful and didn't interrupt our game.

Game over, recess done, we filed back through the doors, up the stairs and into the classroom. The day went by, science, math, lunch, music and then down to the lower level where the art room was.

The art teacher was a free spirit, and she always had some interesting projects for us. There was always music playing, Simon and Garfunkel, Chicago, The Beetles and other popular artists from the day, DJ'd by a couple of classmates. The art room had the smell of turpentine and oil paint lingering in the air. There were pieces of student's artwork hanging on the walls.

The lower level of the school was partially below ground, with big windows that looked out onto the large field in the front of the school. While standing you had a view of the grounds outside. We were working away at our projects listening to "Bridge Over Troubled Water" when we heard things picking up outside. We crowded in front of the windows and standing on tiptoes could see the protesting crowd growing. They were chanting and shouting many of them waving signs. We remained calm but interested in what was going on outside our school. Slowly the crowd approached the flagpole near the front of the school. A couple of long-haired shirtless guys reached the pole, grabbed the halyard and started lowering the flag to half staff. Once at half staff they stepped back and joined the crowd with its chanting, yelling and sign waving.

It was then that something stirred in us, a sort of awakening or calling. Without hesitation or prompting several of us left the art room went up the stairs and outside. We proceeded toward the flagpole through the chaos of the crowd and stopped in front of our school's flag. We fumbled with the halyard then pulled the flag back to full staff. As if in a game, we had captured the flag. We stood in anticipation of some sort of retaliation but there was none. Instead, the crowd fell silent and bowed their heads in prayer. Shameless, we went back inside to art class to work on our projects and listen to music.

The day went on as usual, and the flag remained flying high above our proud school. Soon the bell rang. The day of learning was over.

Once again, I was on my bike, pedaling home.

I never really thought about that day till years later after the truth of that period had been sorted out. Right or wrong we were just kids influenced by the adults and environment in our world. We were doing what we thought needed to be done when we captured the flag.

www.ingramcontent.com/pod-product-compliance
Lightning Source LLC
Chambersburg PA
CBHW041444120626

46547CB00002B/344